This book belongs to

Money Tracker

Date	Detail	Earned	Spent	Total

Money Tracker

Date	Detail	Earned	Spent	Total

Money Tracker

Date	Detail	Earned	Spent	Total

Money Tracker

Date	Detail	Earned	Spent	Total

Money Tracker

Date	Detail	Earned	Spent	Total

Money Tracker

Date	Detail	Earned	Spent	Total

Money Tracker

Date	Detail	Earned	Spent	Total

Money Tracker

Date	Detail	Earned	Spent	Total

Money Tracker

Date	Detail	Earned	Spent	Total

Money Tracker

Date	Detail	Earned	Spent	Total

Money Tracker

Date	Detail	Earned	Spent	Total

Money Tracker

Date	Detail	Earned	Spent	Total

Money Tracker

Date	Detail	Earned	Spent	Total

Money Tracker

Date	Detail	Earned	Spent	Total

Money Tracker

Date	Detail	Earned	Spent	Total

Money Tracker

Date	Detail	Earned	Spent	Total

Money Tracker

Date	Detail	Earned	Spent	Total

Money Tracker

Date	Detail	Earned	Spent	Total

Money Tracker

Date	Detail	Earned	Spent	Total

 # Money Tracker

Date	Detail	Earned	Spent	Total

Money Tracker

Date	Detail	Earned	Spent	Total

Money Tracker

Date	Detail	Earned	Spent	Total

Money Tracker

Date	Detail	Earned	Spent	Total

Money Tracker

Date	Detail	Earned	Spent	Total

Money Tracker

Date	Detail	Earned	Spent	Total

Money Tracker

Date	Detail	Earned	Spent	Total

Money Tracker

Date	Detail	Earned	Spent	Total

Money Tracker

Date	Detail	Earned	Spent	Total

Money Tracker

Date	Detail	Earned	Spent	Total

Money Tracker

Date	Detail	Earned	Spent	Total

Money Tracker

Date	Detail	Earned	Spent	Total

Money Tracker

Date	Detail	Earned	Spent	Total

Money Tracker

Date	Detail	Earned	Spent	Total

Money Tracker

Date	Detail	Earned	Spent	Total

Money Tracker

Date	Detail	Earned	Spent	Total

Money Tracker

Date	Detail	Earned	Spent	Total

Money Tracker

Date	Detail	Earned	Spent	Total

Money Tracker

Date	Detail	Earned	Spent	Total

Money Tracker

Date	Detail	Earned	Spent	Total

Money Tracker

Date	Detail	Earned	Spent	Total

Money Tracker

Date	Detail	Earned	Spent	Total

Money Tracker

Date	Detail	Earned	Spent	Total

Money Tracker

Date	Detail	Earned	Spent	Total

Money Tracker

Date	Detail	Earned	Spent	Total

Money Tracker

Date	Detail	Earned	Spent	Total

Money Tracker

Date	Detail	Earned	Spent	Total

Money Tracker

Date	Detail	Earned	Spent	Total

Money Tracker

Date	Detail	Earned	Spent	Total

Money Tracker

Date	Detail	Earned	Spent	Total

Money Tracker

Date	Detail	Earned	Spent	Total

Money Tracker

Date	Detail	Earned	Spent	Total

Money Tracker

Date	Detail	Earned	Spent	Total

Money Tracker

Date	Detail	Earned	Spent	Total

Money Tracker

Date	Detail	Earned	Spent	Total

Money Tracker

Date	Detail	Earned	Spent	Total

Money Tracker

Date	Detail	Earned	Spent	Total

Money Tracker

Date	Detail	Earned	Spent	Total

Money Tracker

Date	Detail	Earned	Spent	Total

Money Tracker

Date	Detail	Earned	Spent	Total

Money Tracker

Date	Detail	Earned	Spent	Total

Money Tracker

Date	Detail	Earned	Spent	Total

Money Tracker

Date	Detail	Earned	Spent	Total

Money Tracker

Date	Detail	Earned	Spent	Total

Money Tracker

Date	Detail	Earned	Spent	Total

Money Tracker

Date	Detail	Earned	Spent	Total

Money Tracker

Date	Detail	Earned	Spent	Total

Money Tracker

Date	Detail	Earned	Spent	Total

Money Tracker

Date	Detail	Earned	Spent	Total

Money Tracker

Date	Detail	Earned	Spent	Total

Money Tracker

Date	Detail	Earned	Spent	Total

Money Tracker

Date	Detail	Earned	Spent	Total

 # Money Tracker

Date	Detail	Earned	Spent	Total

Money Tracker

Date	Detail	Earned	Spent	Total

Money Tracker

Date	Detail	Earned	Spent	Total

Money Tracker

Date	Detail	Earned	Spent	Total

Money Tracker

Date	Detail	Earned	Spent	Total

Money Tracker

Date	Detail	Earned	Spent	Total

Money Tracker

Date	Detail	Earned	Spent	Total

Money Tracker

Date	Detail	Earned	Spent	Total

Money Tracker

Date	Detail	Earned	Spent	Total

Money Tracker

Date	Detail	Earned	Spent	Total

Money Tracker

Date	Detail	Earned	Spent	Total

Money Tracker

Date	Detail	Earned	Spent	Total

Money Tracker

Date	Detail	Earned	Spent	Total

Money Tracker

Date	Detail	Earned	Spent	Total

Money Tracker

Date	Detail	Earned	Spent	Total

Money Tracker

Date	Detail	Earned	Spent	Total

Money Tracker

Date	Detail	Earned	Spent	Total

Money Tracker

Date	Detail	Earned	Spent	Total

Money Tracker

Date	Detail	Earned	Spent	Total

Money Tracker

Date	Detail	Earned	Spent	Total

Money Tracker

Date	Detail	Earned	Spent	Total

Money Tracker

Date	Detail	Earned	Spent	Total

Money Tracker

Date	Detail	Earned	Spent	Total

Money Tracker

Date	Detail	Earned	Spent	Total

Money Tracker

Date	Detail	Earned	Spent	Total

Money Tracker

Date	Detail	Earned	Spent	Total

 # Money Tracker

Date	Detail	Earned	Spent	Total

Made in the USA
Columbia, SC
24 August 2021